Evidence Against Doubt
Thoughtfully making the case for faith

Evidence Against Doubt

Thoughtfully making the case for faith.

CONTENTS

Why do we wonder?
Evidence from the formation of the universe and the earth.
The Big Bang
Anthropic (Goldilocks) phenomenon
Expansion of the universe
Evidence on the earth
The size of the Earth
The Earth's Atmosphere
Water
Complexity in Nature
Christians

7. Can we know the bible is authentic, has it not been changed and alternative gospel versions destroyed? 45

Prophecy
History
Archaeology
What about 'Alternative Gospels' and Conspiracy theories
What actually happened?
Discoveries of Gnostic codices and texts
Is the Bible a book to be taken literally?
Literary devices and interpreting the bible

PREFACE

For over thirty years I have had the privilege of leading discussion groups for agnostics and Christians with questions.

It seems that there is one question that is so fundamental, so profound, that few of us want to pass through this life without making at least one serious attempt to find the answer.

For if the answer to this question is yes, then our lives have a purpose, there is plan for our lives, we have a future, full of hope, for ourselves, and our loved ones. We have been provided for in every possible way, by someone who has an amazing affection for each of us.

On the other hand if the answer to this question is no, then our lives are simply a biological occurrence, without any particular purpose, and the future of our relatively short lives, depends upon a mixture of human effort, and the laws of chance.

The problem with this question, is that no one can answer it,..... Except you!

Surely some when, we must ask ourselves these questions......Do I believe God Exists?

Is the Bible true?

During the last thirty years I have had the privilege of discussing these questions with many groups of people who were seeking their answer. The following pages are a collection of observations of how rational well educated people answered that question for themselves. This includes the consideration of classic objections to belief in God such as conflict with science and the nature of God.

In several instances I have quoted bible verses which were often used in discussion.

I fully sympathise with those 'questioners' who sometimes feel they are in a sea of circular reasoning

   i.e. Question ... How can I know that God exists?

Answer..... Because the bible says so!

But it is not as simple as that, it is not a blind acceptance of dogma that brought faith, but the open minded consideration of evidence, logic and experience.

Finding faith is a proactive thing, we could spend a life time debating whether we believe sugar is sweet or not,....or we could taste and decide for ourselves!

In discussing classic objections to belief in the existence of God I have set out both sides of the argument in summary form. To set out each in great detail would require a tome which would run the risk of exhausting the reader before they can find those subjects which interest them most. Some may feel I have ignored God's role in bringing people to faith, I haven't. How that works remains to me a mysterious fact which I have seen the outcome of, but could not even begin to try to explain how God effects it.

So all that follows is based upon what I have observed, learned and concluded over 30 years it is for the reader to accept reject or make further study of any of the matters discussed.

Matthew 7:7 ………….. *seek and you will find; knock and the door will be opened to you.*

 Josh Bowmaker
February, 2023

Chapter 1

What they don't teach you in Sunday school

It was one morning over forty years ago that I said to my wife. 'I think it's time we took the boys to Sunday school'. My wife's answer was very profound......... 'Why?'

Neither of us had gone to church regularly since we were teenagers, and now with our boys aged seven and four I was thinking we should. I suppose I wasn't being entirely open, as the truth was I had had some experiences over the previous few years which had repeatedly raised the questions in my mind, do I believe in God, do I believe the bible is true? So I was also interested in going to church myself.

We did start going to church and I joined an adult confirmation class in the hope of getting answers to the many questions I had. A few years later I was recruited as Managing Director of a company based in the north of England so we moved north.

We joined a local church and I was delighted to find that they ran a 'seekers group' where you could seek to get answers to the questions many people have at some time or other.

After two years of attending I was asked if I would lead the group. I have been doing that now for 30 years and have had the privilege discussing and investigating these questions with over 150 people seeking to find or deepen their faith.

One of the most common predicaments is that many of us left Sunday school at junior school age and were taught, understandably, a child appropriate version of Bible stories. In some ways it was 'sugar coated' in the same way as we introduce our children to many other subjects.

The problem comes when we, as adults, find ourselves asking the question 'do I believe in God?' and our reaction is to think back to what we were taught as a child and ask ourselves if we believe that version of the Bible. The answer may often be 'no, not really'.

Basically the issue is we did not complete the course, so we only have the children's version. That is, amongst other things, that everyone in the Bible was either perfect, heroic or both.

The truth is Abraham was a liar, Moses was a murderer, David was an adulterer and an accomplice to murder and Rahab was a prostitute.

What is amazing however is, why and how God chose those people and how he used them to transform the world. These facts are not so significant in finding faith as such, but to many searching adults they have demonstrated how little they knew of what the Bible actually says, and how much more there was to find out; in an adult and objective way.

1 Corinthians 3:1, 2 .... *but as people who are still worldly—mere infants in Christ. I gave you milk, not solid food, for you were not yet ready for it.*

Chapter 2

Belief and understanding- How do we come to believe what we believe?

Some years ago I met a young executive who after many years as a Christian had become a member of his church's leadership team. He was going through what was for him was a crisis. He found that one Sunday without any real warning his faith had simply evaporated. This was a profound shock to him, and as he took time to evaluate what was happening to him he came to a firm conclusion. Thinking deeply and being really honest with himself he came to realise that his 'faith' had in fact never been his, but was that of his parents. It was a faith he had absorbed as if by osmosis. Disappointed and discouraged he left his church and his faith. However within a few months he decided to investigate the validity of the Christian faith for himself, and a couple of years later he discovered a new and personal deep faith in God. So how do we objectively and honestly form our beliefs?

Well text books on Philosophy tell us it is by two means;

1) Rationalism - acquiring belief through logic and reason
2) Empiricism - acquiring beliefs though experience and observation

Apparently the study of understanding and belief is a part of the branch of Philosophy called Epistemology.
In this branch of philosophy 'belief' is defined in two ways;

a) Belief: The state of mind in which a person thinks something to be true, whether they have empirical evidence to prove it or not.

b) 'Justified true belief'; This is defined as meaning, that in order to know that a proposition is true, a person must not only believe the proposition is true, but must also be able to justify his reason for believing so.

In the case of 'faith' we do not have to justify our belief to anyone else, however most people want to justify it in their own mind. That is that their faith is rational to them and based on evidence they accept.

It has been my observation that these two, empiricism and rationalism are the basis on which reasoning intelligent people begin their enquiry regarding belief in God.

Rationalism includes such things as:

- The nature of humans and their existence
- The order and beauty of creation
- Anthropic nature of the universe
- The evidence of prophesy and wisdom in the bible
- Laws e.g. that the laws of thermodynamics suggest a creative power before the 'Big Bang'

Empiricism includes religious experience

- Answers to prayer
- Biblical revelation
- Healing
- Personal revelation
- Transformation of character
- Other personal experiences

Some might question as to whether religious experiences qualify as empirical evidence. I can understand this if they have never had such an experience. It is often true that these experiences are personal and cannot be tested in a scientific sense, but to the individual they are powerful and indisputable evidence of God.

James 4:8   *Come near to God and he will come near to you.*

Do you find God, or does he find you?

The old Hollywood musical 'There's no business like show business' features a love song entitled 'A man chases a girl until she catches him' .
 This apparent contradiction is intended to describe a paradox that most people understand.

In religious thought paradoxes of this type are called 'antinomies', and one of the most famous is the issue of humans having freedom to choose or reject God , alongside the concept of God 'choosing' people to have faith.

The sudden revelation of belief in God, is often called 'A road to Damascus experience', so called because of the nature of the conversion of the apostle Paul described in the Bible.
However whilst I have met several people who have had similar experiences, the majority by far have gone through a progression of inquiry and belief.

Personally I am happy to accept that how God is involved in our discovery of him is a mystery we will never truly understand.

Acts 17: 2-4 *As was his custom, Paul went into the synagogue, and on three Sabbath days he reasoned with them from the Scriptures, 3 explaining and proving that the Messiah had to suffer and rise from the dead. 'This Jesus I am proclaiming to you is the Messiah,' he said. 4 Some of the Jews were persuaded and joined Paul and Silas, as did a large number of God-fearing Greeks and quite a few prominent women.*

Chapter 3.

The Journey of discovery

In the 1975 an American Professor James F Engel, an expert in behavioural science developed a scale which showed thirteen stages of changes in belief that an adult makes, as they progress from atheism to becoming a committed Christian. Many welcomed the work as a helpful way of understanding the issue, some criticised it as being too formulaic.

Whilst I do not claim to have conducted any formal research in the matter, I can say that my observation over thirty years is that for most people who become Christians as adults there does indeed seem to be a pattern to their journey.

Which is:
1) Inquisitive thought
2) Development of interest
3) Investigation of objections
4) Decision

From this starting point the 'belief process' for many believers was typically as follows:

- Firstly The Inquisitive thought: Some experiences or observations caused them to consider the possibility that God may exist.

- Secondly: The development of Interest: They then found conversations or references to the existence of God began to occur or at least be noticed by them.

- Thirdly: Investigation of objections: They begin to investigate and seek answers to scientific, logical, moral or personal objections to belief in God.

- Fourthly: Decision. Having considered the evidence and experience of their investigation they make a decision to take a step of faith or not.

(In my 30 years' experience of leading seekers groups, though I have never kept detailed records,

I would estimate that around 60 % of such seekers found faith, around 30% settle for agnosticism and say around 10% remain atheists.)

Let's look at these phases in the next chapters.

Chapter 4.0

Inquisitive thoughts Phase – Something causes us to wonder

In discussion groups, first meeting conversations often begin with individuals explaining why they decide to join the group.
One young woman described how the experience of standing alone on a cliff top, and viewing the storm lashed seascape, turned her thoughts to wondering about the existence of God.

A young husband explained of how after witnessing the birth of his first child he was deeply moved. It was not just the sense of the 'miraculous' of procreation and birth, but also the instant deep love he felt for his child. This set him to wonder if life had a purpose and there was a God.

It is surely true that everyone at some time in their life wonders if there is a God.

It is Blaise Pascal the brilliant French mathematician and philosopher (1623- 1662) who is credited with putting this into words, he is quoted as saying;

"There is a God-shaped vacuum in the heart of each man which cannot be satisfied by any created thing but only by God the Creator, made know through Jesus Christ."

In fact this is a modern paraphrase of what Pascal actually said but it makes the point, that man suspects there is a God. The Bible make a similar point in the book of Romans 1:20;

For since the creation of the world God's invisible qualities—his eternal power and divine nature—have been clearly seen, being understood from what has been made, so that people are without excuse.

This is saying that simply looking at creation, the earth, the night sky and the beauty all around us that we should realise there is a God.

Another example of our intuitive awareness of God is our instinctive belief in right, wrong and fairness. CS Lewis in his book Mere Christianity gives the illustration of two young children arguing:

They say things like this: 'How'd you like it if anyone did the same thing to you?'—'that's my seat, I was there first'—'Leave him alone, he isn't doing you any harm'— 'Why should you shove in first?' 'Give me a bit of your orange, I gave you a bit of mine'— 'Come on, you promised.'

Even infants without teaching have a sense of right, wrong and fairness within them.
As the Bible says:

Romans 2:14-16 (The Message)
14-16 When outsiders who have never heard of God's law follow it more or less by instinct, they confirm its truth by their obedience. They show that God's law is not something alien, imposed on us from without, but woven into the very fabric of our creation. There is something deep within them that

echoes God's yes and no, right and wrong. Their response to God's yes and no will become public knowledge on the day God makes his final decision about every man and woman.

Imagine that you arrive at your home unexpectedly. You open the front door and call out 'Hello is anybody Home' but you receive no reply. You were calling out to nobody, but you were not behaving irrationally or illogically. You had enough experience and evidence to consider it was a possibility someone would answer.

It is of course necessary, by definition to believe in the possibility of the existence of God in order to make sense of attempting to enquire about him. Some may argue that this is tautological (circular) reasoning but it is not. However the illustrations given in the previous pages apply, and are no different to the logic of developing a hypothesis in engineering and science.

That is that a hypothesis is imagined or considered as a possibility, it is subjected to research, evidence gathering testing etc. and finally judged to be a truth or otherwise.

How then, do rational thinking well educated people come to the conclusion that God not only exists, but that it is both beneficial and fundamental to a fulfilled life, to have a relationship with him?

In my experience people begin this journey for one of five reasons; (I am sure there are others!)

1.   They experience recurrent nagging questions that inexplicably keep coming to mind over the years. Does God exists? What is the purpose of my life?

2.   They observe the beauty, complexity and intricacy of the world, life and the universe, and wonder if there is a creator.

3.   They experience a significant event in life, negative or positive which causes them to wonder about God.

4.   An observed fundamental change in a friend or loved one who themselves have come to faith, which causes the observer to consider what has caused the change.

5.   They hear a sermon or read a book which causes them to want to know more.

People are different! Very different!
A friend of mine who was research scientist with Masters Degrees and a Ph.D. in Bio- chemistry, Pharmacology and Computer science had always dismissed the existence of God as irrational.

One day, at a friend's invitation, he attended a church service. During the singing of a modern hymn one verse spoke of the nature of God, and this caused him to experience deep emotions. This indeed he felt was completely irrational, totally outside his experience but at the same time very real. He had a sense 'something' trying to communicate with him'. This began his questioning phase.

Others having similar experiences may find themselves unmoved and their default thoughts, would be these experiences were a mixture of coincidence and emotional state.

Some physicists and mathematicians are in awe of how the language of mathematics seems able to describe every aspect of the known universe. It is as if the whole universe is a complex mathematical model that one day will reveal that 'theory of everything'. Such amazing calculable conformity has moved many to consider the possibility of God's existence.

Others having witnessed the selfless action of a committed believer, find themselves wondering if that person's God could be real.

The questions and experiences which may turn our thoughts to God are many and varied.

These experiences are not proof in themselves but often raise the question of God's existence in our mind. Thousand of people can testify to this:

Here are just some common experiences which can cause us to enter the questioning phase:

- Nature and the universe
- Our Existence
- Anthropic phenomena within the universe (Explained in Chapter 7.1)
- Child birth
- Nature of love
- Beauty of science and mathematics
- A bereavement
- The effect of art and music on the human spirit
- The existence of mathematical forms in nature
- The changed personality of a converted person
- An answered prayer or apparent miracle

Chapter 5.0

Developing interest Phase - Recurring thoughts and reminders

Most people have probably had some kind of 'Does God exist?' moment like those described in the preceding paragraphs even if ever so fleeting.

However it is often reported amongst people who eventually come to believe in God that following that 'fleeting moment' over the following weeks and months they experience an increased occurrence of references to God and the question of his existence.

Now you can put this down to the fact that they have sensitised themselves to the subject by their recent experience or this is some kind of divine intervention.

The choice is yours, all I can say is that this was my own experience and of many believers I have counselled. In fact so common a phenomena is it that amongst Christians the word 'Godincidence' rather than coincidence is often used.

My own experience though comprising seemingly trivial events came with such frequency and timing as to be very thought provoking.

Days after entertaining the question 'Does God Exist?' I was in a book shop looking for a book on World War 2 naval history, right in front of me and completely misfiled in the wrong section was a book entitled 'A new life a new life style'.

I flicked through the pages thinking it was about career change or starting a business. It was in fact a book about becoming a Christian.

It talked of the existence of God which of course and fuelled further questions in my mind.
However my overriding thought was that this was a remarkable and interesting coincidence. With fairly rapid succession several other incidents occurred.

In my early career in my job capacity as an Operations Manager in a manufacturing company, I received a complaint that one of our employees was 'Bible Bashing' and upsetting colleagues.

In dealing with the issue I found the allegations to be untrue and unfair. However the issue had arisen when a colleague had asked the so called 'Bible Basher' Do you believe in God?

So in dealing with an HR problem between two employees, the question of God's existence was brought to my mind yet again.

Several similar albeit minor incidences later I began to be intrigued by the level of coincidence and the recurrence of the question 'Do you believe God exists?'

As these thoughts kept returning to my mind it led me on to a decision to seriously investigate this question for myself.
For over 30 years now I have been leading discussions small groups of people who have

arrived at this point of 'investigation' by the same or very similar route.

Chapter 6.0

The Investigation Phase – What is it I don't believe and why?

Is the issue I am struggling with actually in the Bible?

Having decided they wish to investigate the question 'Does God Exist?' many people wonder where to start. Today there are many courses such as the 'Alpha Course', but formulaic courses are not for everyone, particularly in the early phase of investigation. Though we may share the process of discovery the specific 'barriers to belief' vary from person to person.

Having said that in my experience of many years the most often raised 'barriers to belief' are expressed as follows:

'I believe there may be some greater power, but I have many issues I need to resolve, for example:

- Is there actually any evidence that God exists
- Can we know the bible is authentic, has it not been changed and alternative gospels destroyed?
- Science has proved the Bible is wrong about the age of the earth.
- Science has proved that the earth was not made in six days
- Science has proved that evolution not God created animals and humans
- The bible is full of unbelievable accounts and contradictions
- The Bible says God is a God of love yet in the Old Testament he commands and condones violence and bloodshed.
- The Bible was written by men and is composed of mythical stories, and has been changed to present them as truth
- Why does God allow suffering if he is a God of love?
- Why would God make rules about sex and sexuality?

In the next chapters I summarise the responses and discussions which seem to have provided help to many people seeking answers to the above questions.

Is there any evidence that God exists

Some years ago I was called for Jury service, in a criminal case of serial burglaries.
 I was asked to be the foreman of the Jury, and when we had heard all of the evidence, the Judge sent we twelve members of the jury to deliberate. He told us that he would accept a majority verdict of 10 to 2, but we must consider the evidence and conclude 'beyond reasonable doubt' whether the defendant was guilty or not. Unfortunately no one had witnessed the defendant carrying out the burglaries so the only evidence was 'circumstantial'. For example he was found in possession of some of the stolen items, his shoe print was found near the garden of a burgled house. However this and other 'circumstantial 'evidence could not prove beyond <u>any</u> doubt that he was the burglar.

Initially the jury was split 7 to 5 but after several hours of discussion a majority of 11 to 1 was achieved and the defendant was found guilty.

The Jury could never know with absolute certainty that the defendant was guilty, but we believed he was, in our evaluation, guilty beyond reasonable doubt.

In trying to answer the question of God's existence the same criteria apply, and it is without question that circumstantial evidence exists, but it also true that only the jury (you) can decide.

So here is some evidence.

Why do we wonder?

Firstly surely one of the greatest pieces of evidence that God exists is the fact that most of us ask ourselves if he does!

Why in a purely chemically created random world would so many of us keep wondering if there is a God. Why would it even cross our mind, unless the thought was put there?

Even atheists seem obsessed with the idea, they continue to debate and show interest in the possibility of the idea.

If someone told me that they believed in fairies, I would accept that they did believe that, but I would not spend months writing books trying to prove them wrong.

Much can be learned from the atheist's writings and arguments. These could be typified as follows:

I believe in evolution therefore God does not exist! So what if God created evolution. Or, I don't believe in God because of all the suffering in the world. This is like saying I do not agree with how my Prime minister or President behaves therefore I do not believe he exists!
Surely any reasonable person would acknowledge that the idea of the possibility God's existence seems to have been programmed within us.
This was most famously observed by the French philosopher and mathematician Blaise Pascal, as mentioned in a previous chapter.

'"There is a God-shaped vacuum in the heart of each man which cannot be satisfied by any created thing but only by God the Creator, made know through Jesus Christ."

Evidence from the formation of the universe and the earth.

The Big Bang

The theory that the universe was created by a massive explosion, often referred to as the 'Big Bang' is fairly well known.

The energy required to cause creation (Big Bang or otherwise) was massive billions and billions and billions of megatons.

However if you cast your mind back to your school physics lessons you might recall the first law of thermodynamics states that energy can neither be created nor destroyed. So where did this energy for the 'Big Bang' come from?

This energy could not have existed within the universe because science has proved that the universe did not always exist.

So some incredible source of power existed before the universe was created. Christians believe this eternal omnipotent force is God.

Anthropic (Goldilocks) phenomenon
In the childrens story of 'Goldilocks and the three bears' Goldilocks tries three bowls of porridge, one is too hot, one too cold and third 'just right' . The so called 'Anthropic principle' is nick named the 'Goldilocks principle' because it describes phenomena existing in the universe which are just perfect to support the existence of the earth and life upon it. Some of these are so precisely ordered they are staggering, for example.

Expansion of the universe
After the 'Big Bang' the universe expanded; if the rate of expansion was marginally slower than it actually was it would have collapsed back on itself. If it had been any faster then the chemicals and atomic structures we and our earth are all made would not have had time to form.

The size of the Earth

The Earth's size and corresponding gravity holds a thin layer of gases, only extending about 50 miles above the Earth's surface. If Earth were smaller, an atmosphere would be impossible.

If the Earth were larger, its atmosphere would be un-breathable.

The Earth's Atmosphere

Earth is the only known planet equipped with an atmosphere of the right mixture of gases to sustain plant, animal and human life.

Our atmosphere is composed of 78% nitrogen, 21% oxygen, and .03% carbon dioxide. If oxygen made up 23% or 19%, there could be no life on earth.

Water

Water is a universal solvent. This means that thousands of chemicals, minerals and nutrients can be carried throughout our bodies and into the smallest blood vessels.

Water has a unique surface tension. Water in plants can therefore flow upward against gravity, bringing life-giving water and nutrients to the top of even the tallest trees.

Water is the only substance which gets lighter as it freezes because of this the sea does not freeze from the bottom up; if it did life could not exist.

Trees and plants

Humans breathe in oxygen and exhale CO_2 whist trees and vegetation absorb CO_2 and 'breathe out' oxygen giving a mutually sustainable life cycle.

These are just a few of hundreds of anthropic phenomena known to science.

Complexity in Nature

The sheer beauty and complexity of nature, conception and birth of children, the body's ability to heal itself etc etc, cause many people to think that there is a designer of the universes and earth.

Christians

There are throughout the world 4.3 billion people, over 50 % of the words population, who believe in the God of the Old Testament. Surely if half the people of the world say they have seen enough evidence to believe in God it must be worthy of serious consideration.

Chapter 7

Can we know the bible is authentic? Has it not been changed and alternative gospel versions destroyed as some claim?

There is a massive amount of evidence to confirm the authenticity of the Bible and that it has been handed down unaltered for example. The Dead Sea Scrolls are probably the most famous manuscript discovered. They were found in 1947 in a cave at Qumran. They are 2000 years old and contain hand written copies of almost every book of the Old Testament, comparison with modern copies show that the text and content has been accurately handed down over that time.

In addition to this the authenticity of the Bible is supported by the following

Prophecy
There are hundreds of prophecies in the bible which have already come true. Isaiah 53, is just

one example. There are 38 prophesies in the Old Testament about the coming messiah, that the new testament writers point out came true in the coming and life of Jesus.

History
Evidence from the writings of non-Christian Jewish and Roman historians, such as Josephus, Tacitus, Pliny etc.

One example from 'Antiquities of the Jewish People', written by Josephus in 93 AD reads

'Now, there was a man about this time Jesus, a wise man, if it be lawful to call him a man, for he was a doer of wonderful works, a teacher of such men as receive the truth with pleasure. He drew over to him both many of the Jews, and many of the Gentiles. He was the Christ. And when Pilate, at the suggestion of the principal men amongst us, had condemned him to the cross, those that loved him at the first did not forsake him; for he appeared to them alive again on the third day; as the divine prophets

had foretold these and ten thousand other wonderful things concerning him. And the tribe of Christians, so named from him, are not extinct at this day.

Archaeology
Archaeological digs are continually confirming biblical facts, characters and events.

Example -- Because the town of Nazareth is never mentioned in the Old Testament experts stated that term 'Jesus of Nazareth' must be incorrect.
 Excavations in 1955 demonstrated that a town called Nazareth did after all exist.
Such revelations of evidence have continued down the years.

What about 'Alternative Gospels' and Conspiracy theories?
Some television programmes and books have claimed that alternative gospel accounts exist

and these have been destroyed or hidden by the church.

The reports are presented as if an ancient conspiracy had been uncovered. This is a complete fallacy in that all the 'gospel' accounts referred to are well known are in the public domain (even bookshops).

The actual history of these matters is as follows:
The majority of these writings are known as the 'Gnostic Writings' Gnosticism is very ancient and is a combination of philosophy and religion.

It is very broad and various in concept and therefore difficult to define.

Its origins are not really known. What is known for certain is that it is a syncretic religion. That is a religion which adapts and adopts other religious ideas of the societies within which it exists.

It has been likened to Buddhism or Zoroastrianism (Iran). Hindu and Brahmanism are also current examples where followers are free to 'borrow' from other religions.

What actually happened?

Following the writing of the Gospels by Matthew, Mark, Luke and John, Gnostics and others began to adopt some parts of the Christian Gospel and 'syncretise' it with their existing beliefs.

The word Gnosis from which Gnosticism comes means 'Knowledge'.
A core part of Gnosticism is that one requires special knowledge to achieve salvation, and parts of that knowledge are secret and communicated only between adherents.
This can be seen in the gnostic writings titles such as The <u>Secret</u> Gospel of Thomas, The Secret Gospel of 'whoever'. Thus implying that there is inner secret knowledge which only they know about. These writings began to circulate

in the late first century and the Bible writes warnings about them

1 Timothy 6:20-21
20 Timothy, guard what has been entrusted to your care. Turn away from godless chatter and the opposing ideas of what is falsely called knowledge (Gnosticism), 21 which some have professed and in so doing have departed from the faith.
Grace be with you all.

Faced with a growing number of cults and what they believed to be their heretical writings, the early church leaders began a campaign to produce a list of authorised scriptures called the canon.

Much Gnostic writing is written to negate or contradict an existing belief or idea.
In other words by definition something existed (Christians would say the truth) before the negation can be written.

Particular examples are that most of the attributes of Jesus Christ written in the New Testament are negated and reversed in Gnostic writings. e.g. Jesus never sinned versus Jesus had a very sinful childhood. Jesus rose from the dead versus Jesus had a twin brother who was substituted for him and so it goes on.

Discoveries of Gnostic codices and texts

Although there were references to Gnostic writings by early church few full versions existed.
However in 1945 an amazing discovery was made in what is known as the Nag Hammadi Library.
The Nag Hammadi library is a collection of early Christian and Gnostic texts discovered near the Upper Egyptian town of Nag Hammadi in 1945.

Thirteen leather-bound vellum codices buried in a sealed jar were found by a local farmer. These writings comprised of fifty-two mainly

Gnostic books. Probably the best-known of these works is the Gospel of Thomas.

Many of these 'gospels' have been available in modern print for many years and are not a new revelation, nor has research resulted in giving them any credibility as orthodox Christian writings.

It is true that the Catholic and Orthodox Bibles include some books which are not in the protestant bible. The reason for this is as follows:

The Catholic Old Testament includes the books of Tobit, Judith, The Book of Wisdom, Sirach (also called Ecclesiaticus), Baruch, 1 Maccabees, and 2 Maccabees, which the modern protestant bible does not have.

No one disputes that these books are genuine accounts written at the time between the Old Testament and the New Testament. However the issue was, were they the 'Word of God' or well written history.

Originally these seven books were in all bibles however during the sixteenth century Martin Luther a German Theologian and priest proposed that these books should be put in an appendix of the bible and not in the Old Testament itself.

His argument for doing so was:

1.   Christ and the Apostles never quoted from these books as they do others.

2.   None of the books of these books claim to be scripture, by saying 'this is the word of God', or by describing anointed prophets or prophecy.

3.   The author of some books (e.g. Maccabees) interprets the events not as a miraculous intervention by God, but rather God's using the instrument of the military genius of the Maccabees to achieve his ends.

This therefore reads more like history than inspired scripture.

The historical accuracy of these books is well proven, and they are very interesting to read, however over the years, modern protestant bibles have left out the appendix of these seven books, so it has to be bought separately, or as part of the Catholic bible.

So the existence of the two canons of scripture is not some big conspiracy, but simply a genuinely held view that the seven books in question are history and not the inspired word of God.

Both are available very widely and any individual can read and study them.

CONCLUSION: There are many excellent books describing research which proves that the bible is authentic and has come down to us unaltered.

As the Bible says in Luke 1:1-4

1 Many have undertaken to draw up an account of the things that have been fulfilled among us, 2 just as they were handed down to us by those who from the first were eyewitnesses and servants of the word. 3 With this in mind, since I myself have carefully investigated everything from the beginning, I too decided to write an orderly account for you, most excellent Theophilus, 4 so that you may know the certainty of the things you have been taught.

Is the Bible a book to be taken literally?

According to the Bible 'If your right eye causes you to stumble, gouge it out and throw it away'

Seems extreme! But this is hyperbole, which is a deliberate exaggeration to make a point.

A careful study of the text shows that it means ' if looking at something you shouldn't, causes you to do something you shouldn't, then stop looking.

Before deciding to criticise or reject the Bible it is essential to find out about the way it's written in order to give it a fair trial.

A question often asked in the early days of a discussion group is 'Do Christians take the Bible literally?'

My answer would be 'only the literal bits'.

When reading the Bible misunderstandings can occur if we are not fully aware of the literary devices it uses.

Most people are familiar with the more common ones such as a 'parable', that is a fictional story composed to illustrate a truth.

However there are many others, and being aware of them helps us understand and interpret what the bible is saying

Literary devices and interpreting the bible

The bible contains prose written as an author, journalist, historian or teacher would write, when

this is seen there is no reason for special interpretation.
If it makes literal sense and it is clear the writer intends it to be literal then it is wrong to try to re-interpret it.

However there are over 20 literary devices used in the bible which are not meant to be taken literally; here are some of the most common;

Figures of speech and idiom
Modern examples
It's raining cats and dogs outside.
If that happens, I will eat my hat.

Figures of speech in the Bible
Matthew 23; 24; You blind guides! You strain out a gnat but swallow a camel.
Isaiah 55:12; the mountains and hills will burst into song before you,
and all the trees of the field will clap their hands.

Parables

A story told to reveal a moral or spiritual truth e.g. Parables of the sower and The Good Samaritan

Poetry

The English poet Tennyson wrote a famous poem about an ill-fated cavalry charge in the Battle of Balaclava, entitled 'The charge of the Light Brigade'. It is a poetic account of a factual event. It includes expressions which are not literally true but written with poetic license. However it speaks some absolute truths; that the charge should not have been ordered, that the soldiers were loyal and brave, that their lives were wasted.

Anyone reading the poem would understand these points, and reading the history could find the factual account.

The poem was written to be thought provoking and to be memorised.

There is much poetry in the bible which when translated into English from Hebrew is more difficult to recognise.

Poetry was used as in modern language to add, depth of meaning and feeling. It was also used to aid memorisation of scripture.

Hyperbole

An extravagant statement or figure of speech not intended to be taken literally, as "to wait an eternity ".

Genesis 22:17 I will surely bless you and make your descendants as numerous as the stars in the sky and as the sand on the seashore.

Euphemism

A polite word used in place of a potentially offensive one...

John 11:11 "Our friend Lazarus has fallen asleep; but I am going there to wake him up." (John 11:11)

Several words are used as euphemisms for male and female private parts and sexual relations etc.

e.g... Adam <u>knew</u> his wife... Foot, or thigh in place of sexual organs.

'To uncover someone's nakedness' originally meant the act of consummation of husband and wife, but is used in scripture as a euphemism for various sexual acts.

Polysemy

Words which are spelt the same but have a range of meaning.

The word for "day" is the Hebrew word, "yom." It can mean:

The period of light (contrasted from the period of darkness).

A twenty four hour period.

A general vague "time".

A point in time.

A year.

Acrostic

This is a device found in Old Testament psalms and poetry in which the successive lines of a poem

begin with the consecutive letters of the Hebrew alphabet.
It was done to help students memorise the text.

Obviously there may be some poetic licence in regard to choosing words to accommodate the acrostic. Also when translated the alphabetic acrostic is lost.

Imagery
This is the use of vivid or figurative language to represent objects, actions, or ideas.
Revelation 12:1, "Now a great sign appeared in heaven: a woman clothed with the sun, with the moon under her feet, and on her head a garland of twelve stars."
This imagery is reminiscent of Joseph's dream of the sun, moon, and stars in Genesis 37:9.

Paradox
This is a statement that seems to be illogical or contradictory on the surface, but actually conveys a deeper truth.

Matthew 16:25, "For whoever desires to save his life will lose it, but whoever loses his life for My sake will find it."

Symbolism

A symbol is a representation, token or sign. It is something that stands for or suggests something else.

The Bible contains a great deal of symbolism and symbolic language which can be numbers, actions, or objects. These need to be studied to understand their meaning, which is not literal.

So, many people are often struggling to believe, writings in the bible which they were never expected to take literally. So it can be helpful to seek advice sometimes.

Chapter 8

Science has proved the Bible is wrong about the age of the earth, therefore can we rely on its accuracy in general?

This view is quite commonly held but the fact is that nowhere in the Bible does it state how old the earth is or when it was created.

What has happened down the centuries is that various scholars have tried to 'calculate' an age of the earth based upon other facts contained within the Bible. To this day there is no firm agreement amongst Christians about the issue. Below is a comparison of Christian and scientific views of the age of the earth together with some criticisms.

Alternative Christian interpretation

A Young Earth

Many Christians believe that the age of the earth can be calculated by adding up the ages of people mentioned in the Bibles lists of ancestors (genealogies) from Adam and Eve onward.

This gives an age of the earth to be about 6000 years.

Criticism:

a) Biblical genealogies were not intended to be used in this way, and some only record 'famous' people, thereby leaving significant gaps.

b) Geological studies seem to show a 6000 year age is too young.

Old Earth

Genesis 1:1-2
The beginning

1 In the beginning God created the heavens and the earth. 2 Now the earth was formless and empty, darkness was over the surface of the deep, and the Spirit of God was hovering over the waters.
Another Christian interpretation is that the first verse in the Bible which says 'In the beginning God

64

created the heavens and the earth'. Is simply a statement of what God did and it doesn't tell us when he did it.

That act could have taken billions of years. The next verses go on to describe an earth which exists as a barren wilderness, waiting to be made habitable.
Second verse. 'Now the earth was formless and empty............
Based upon this the age of the earth is unknown and could be billions of years.

Criticism:
a) This view was developed to harmonise the bible with Geology. (Actually this interpretation is centuries old and before Geology existed)

Scientific dating of the age of the earth

Geological Column
The geological column is based upon the idea that the earth's crust is composed of a series of layers (strata) deposited and formed over centuries.

Using this as a dating method was proposed by Charles Lyell a Scottish lawyer, in the 1830's.

Amongst other things it uses fossils found in the different strata to determine the age of the strata. (See illustration below).

Millions of years ago	Period of Geological Column Stata	Type of animal fossils according to evolutionary theory
2	Quaternary	Human
65	Tertiary	Primitive horse
130	Cretaceous	Last Dinosaurs
180	Jurassic	Dinosaurs
225	Triassic	First Dinosaurs
275	Permian	Reptiles
345	Carboniferous	Insects
405	Devonian	Fishes
435	Silurian	Molluscs
480	Ordovician	Brachiopods
600	Cambrian	Trilobites

Criticism:
a) The method uses fossils to estimate the date of strata, the age of the fossil being estimated from evolutionary theory. Some suggest this is using one hypothesis to try and prove another hypothesis and is therefore unsound.

b) The earth's strata in the form of a geological column is not found all over the earth.

c) Disruption of strata though earthquake, volcanic action, and floods etc. make accurate dating improbable.

Radiometric Dating

Radiometric dating is a scientific technique geologists use to establish the age of rocks.
It works by measuring the result of radioactivity in rocks and minerals.
You will recall from science studies at school that all matter is composed of atoms.
Atoms are the smallest bit of matter that can be identified. (or as the Bible says...' the universe was

formed at God's command, so that what is seen was not made out of what was visible'. Hebrews 11:3).

Atoms comprise of a nucleus surrounded by orbiting electrons a bit like the sun being orbited by planets.

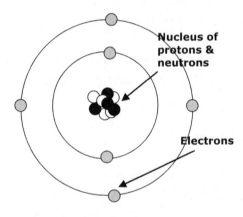

Nucleus of protons & neutrons

Electrons

The nucleus in the centre comprises of extremely small particles (sub atomic particles) called protons and neutrons. The number of protons in the nucleus determine what the type of matter or element the substance is. For example an atom with six protons is an atom of the element carbon, and an atom having seven protons is an atom of nitrogen. If the number of protons remains the same but the number of neutrons varies a variant of the element is formed called an isotope.

As an example of this is carbon which has three common isotopes.

Carbon 12 has six neutrons and six protons
Carbon 13 has seven neutrons and six protons
Carbon 14 has eight neutrons and six protons

In regard to rocks and minerals some isotopes formed are unstable and do not remain as the original element, but through a process of decay become a different element.

This change occurs at a constant rate known as radioactive decay. So if the decay rate is known it can be used to measure the age of a specimen of rock.

As an example a certain type of uranium will, by a series of steps, slowly decay into lead. In measuring the status of this change in a rock sample a calculation of the rock's age can be made.

In radiometric terminology the original uranium is called the 'parent' element and lead is called the 'daughter' element.
It is assumed that when created the rock would contain 100% of the parent element and as it 'decayed' this would progressively change to the daughter element of lead.

So if the ratio of parent to daughter is known then the age of the rock can be calculated

The rate of change from parent to daughter is measure in 'half-lives' that is the time it takes for the percentage of parent to halve.

As an illustration this is shown graphically for Uranium -238 which has a half- life of 4.5 billion years.

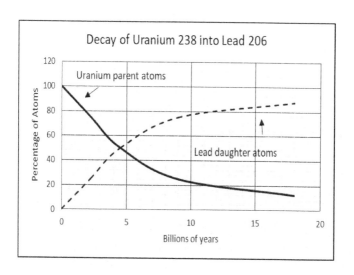

Decay of Uranium 238 into Lead 206

So the graph shows that every 4.5 billion years the proportion of parent atoms changes from 100% to 50% to 25% and so on.

Criticism:

a) It is claimed that In many validation experiments radiometric dating has failed to measure accurately, rocks of 'known' ages'.

b) The technique is based upon assumptions, firstly that the rocks being analysed had 100% parent atoms and zero daughter when created. Secondly that the decay rate has been constant and has never varied (as represented by the smooth graph) for billions of years. Thirdly that no parent or daughter atoms have entered or left the rock during intrusion or melting etc. due to action of volcanoes, earthquakes or subduction (i.e. geological action at tectonic plate boundaries).

CONCLUSION: The Age of the earth is not known for certain. The Bible does not anywhere state the age of the earth. For many people it is hard to accept that, for radiometric dating purposes, 'assuming' the atomic structure of rocks existing 4.5 billion years ago is not sound.

Perhaps the age of the earth will never be known with certainty.

There is no doubt much yet to discover and learn however it does not seem reasonable to reject the

Bible or belief in God because of the existence of arguments about the age of the earth.

Chapter 9

Science has proved that the earth was not made in six days

Before we try to answer this question here are two very interesting facts to ponder

a) That science and the Bible basically agree on the order of creation.

b) That probability of them agreeing by chance is 87 billion to one.

Order of creation
1. Light (stars), Gen. 1:3
2. Sun formed, Gen. 1:4
3. Earth formed, Gen. 1:6-9
4. Oceans, water, Gen. 1:10
5. Grasses, Gen. 1:11
6. Herbs, Gen. 1:11
7. Seed-bearing plants, Gen. 1:11
8. Trees, Gen. 1:11
9. Sky clearing, to see sun and moon, Gen. 1-14

10. Fishes, Gen. 1:20
11. Birds, Gen. 1:20
12. Small land creatures, Gen. 1:24
13. Cattle, large land animals, Gen. 1:24
14. Man, Gen. 1:26

Probability of science and the Bible agreeing by chance:

In writing the Bible, any human writer had 14 possibilities to choose from for his first event.
Now, for his SECOND event, he has 13 remaining options to choose from, so he could pick any of those thirteen, and so on.
This choosing process would continue for each remaining event.
The total number of combinations that a human writer could have written down is therefore 14 x 13 x 12 x 11 x 10 x 9 x 8 x 7 x 6 x 5 x 4 x 3 x 2 x 1 or what mathematicians call 14 factorial.

This is an incredibly huge number! It is 87,178,291,200.

A human writer then, without God's Inspiration, could actually have written the creation sequence in Genesis in 87 billion different ways!

That is, it is 87 billion to 1 chance for science and bible to accidently agree

So back to our question. Was the earth created in seven 24 hour days? First let us look at Christian interpretations of the Bible.

Alternative Christian interpretations

Literal six 24 hour days

Many Christians hold the view that the seven days (6 days of creation 7th day God rested) mentioned in the first book of the Bible (Genesis) are literally seven 24 hour days.

Criticism:

This interpretation seems to be at odds with the 'evidence' of geology and evolution theory.

2) The days in Genesis mentioned are not 24 hour days but much longer passages of time.

This view is based upon the interpretation of the original Hebrew word used when the Old Testament was first written.

The Hebrew word for day is 'Yom' and it can mean a:

- Period of light (as contrasted with the period of darkness),
- Period of twenty-four hours
- General term for time
- Point of time
- Sunrise to sunset
- Sunset to next sunset
- A year
- Time period of unspecified length.
- A long, but finite span of time - age - epoch - season.

A modern example of similar use of the word 'day' would be 'In Julius Caesar's 'day' ships had no engines, and were at the mercy of wind and tide.'

The scientific view of the duration of 'creation' is largely determined by the theory of evolution which is addressed in the next chapter.

CONCLUSION: If God is powerful enough to create the whole universe, then he would not be constrained by time. (That is if time existed at creation).

Understandably much effort and scholarship is put into semantics, translation of words of bible texts, but whether the Hebrew word 'Yom' means an 'age' or 24 hour day does not impact on the essential teaching of the Bible.
 Based on this it does not seem reasonable to reject the Bible or belief in God because of the existence of differing interpretations of the duration of creation.

Chapter 10

Science has proved that evolution not God created animals and humans

This is a huge subject and it would seem to be the motion of a never ending debate.
There are basically two Christian views on the issue of evolution versus creation.

Alternative Christian interpretations

1) Evolution is an unproven theory, and is wrong as it contradicts the bible.

2) Evolution was part of the way God ordered creation.
  Some Christians believe that God used evolution as part of his creative process. They cite the bible verse Genesis 1:24 as God's command for evolution to take place. The verses reads:

24 And God said, 'Let the land produce living creatures according to their kinds: the livestock, the creatures that move along the ground, and the wild animals, each according to its kind.' And it was so.

Scientific view.

Theory of Evolution

Science hypothesises that all life began by chance. Beginning with simplest of life forms, random mutations within living cells caused genetic change giving some advantage in survival. This phenomenon repeated countless times progressively gave a perpetual development of species through the survival of the fittest, and other mechanisms.

Criticism:
Evolution is a complex subject with continual modifications to the theory, however most criticism can be grouped under the following summaries:

a) Some critics believe that the mathematical probability of the process of evolution and a single cell evolving into a complex human being so low as to be considered 'impossible' in statistical terms.

b) Secondly the huge passage of time required to bring about speciation and change, means that the 'favourable conditions' giving benefit to a mutation would need to persist for millions of years and this is not feasible.

c) There is no indisputable scientific evidence to prove the theory of evolution

d) Some animals and biological systems demonstrate 'irreducible complexity'. That is, they have complex multifunctional abilities which could not have evolved sequentially. All features would be needed simultaneously in order to exist or give any advantage.
Taking simplistic analogy. If a car engine suddenly evolved it would provide no advantage until it was connected to fuel,

gearbox, wheels and body etc. the chance of these interacting components evolving at the same time through random mutation is not plausible.

Examples cited of irreducible complexity in biology are the human eye, and various species. One example is the Bombardier Beetle which when threatened by a predator fires two chemicals from two separate tubes at its rear end. When these two chemicals mix they explode warding off the predator. It uses inlet and exhaust valves to control the chemicals. If the chemicals mixed inside the beetle it would explode. The beetle has to produce to hazardous chemicals (hydrogen peroxide and hydroquinone). It then aims the explosive stream at its predator using a movable nozzle. All of these features would have had to evolve simultaneously and rapidly, if disaster for the beetle is to be avoided.

It is argued that this complexity and other factors suggest 'intelligent design'.

e) Fossils found in strata in the Geological Column are used as evidence for dating and evolutionary change. However analysis shows that before the Cambrian period there are few fossils but during it there is a sudden proliferation of species of all kinds. This sudden existence of species is known as the Cambrian Explosion. Critics of evolutionary theory argue that this is evidence that life began simultaneously for hundreds of species and not in the slow sequential manner that evolutionary theory claims.

Proposed Evolutionary pattern of growth and diversity

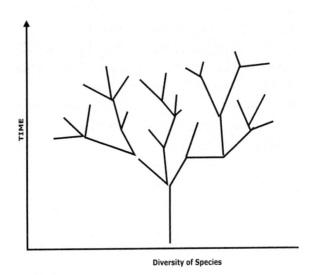

TIME

Diversity of Species

Actual pattern of growth and diversity 'Cambrian Explosion' (As found in Fossils)

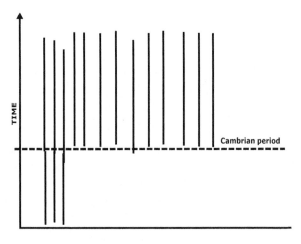

Diversity of Species

CONCLUSION: The theory of evolution may or may not be based on fact, however if it is true there is no evidence to suggest that evolution was not a creative act of God.

Based on this it does not seem reasonable to reject the Bible or belief in God because of the existence of evolutionary theory.

Chapter 11

**The Bible says God is a God of love yet in the
Old Testament God commands
and condones violence and bloodshed.**

This is a common issue for many people but we
have to realise God did not want these things to
happen. In fact he pleaded with his chosen people
in many attempts to avoid them. Also not all acts of
violence in the Bible are approved of by God, many
incidence are recorded simply as historical events.
The basic facts are that God made contracts
(covenants) with the people of Israel which they
willingly agreed to abide by.
He chose them to be the people through whom he
would reveal his existence, and also reveal his
desire for faith in him, to the whole world.

He also swore that through them he would bring a
Messiah into the world to change it forever.

All he asked them to do was:

- Believe in him and teach their children to believe in him.
- To obey his commandments and set a moral example to the world, so they would know what he was like.
- To spread belief in God wherever they travelled.
- Not to worship idols or to make new religions
- Be a moral and religious nation through whom God could bring Jesus into the world.

In return God promised that if the people of Israel kept their side of the contract he would:
(Paraphrased from Deuteronomy 28)

- Bless their whole land city and country
- Bless their children
- Provide for them
- He would bless their businesses and make them prosperous
- Any enemies who rose up against them would be defeated

- He will establish them as Holy people
- All people on earth will realise you are God's chosen people
- He would bring forth the messiah (Jesus) through them

However if they did not keep their word, all of the above would be reversed into curses not blessings.

Now God keeps his word! As the Bible tells us for example in Isaiah 46:10-11

10 I make known the end from the beginning, from ancient times, what is still to come.
I say, 'My purpose will stand, and I will do all that I please.' 11 From the east I summon a bird of prey; from a far-off land, a man to fulfil my purpose.
What I have said, that I will bring about; what I have planned, that I will do.

So throughout the Old Testament If the people of Israel remained faithful to God he protected them, and if that required the defeat of an invading army by warfare he facilitated it, often giving victory when Israel was hopelessly outnumbered.

On the other hand at the times the people of Israel drifted from belief in and worship of God, he acted to stop the decline. When disbelief was common and only few believers left he acted powerfully to ensure that belief in him and the coming Messiah did not die out altogether.

This included using Israel's enemies to reduce their numbers by warfare, and taking into captivity the believing remnant. This remnant would be later released and used by God to restore belief and worship in Israel.

God never acted without warning he sent prophets to plead with and warn the people.
For example:

Jeremiah 3:12-13
*12 Go, proclaim this message towards the north:
'"Return, faithless Israel," declares the Lord,*

*"I will frown on you no longer, for I am faithful,"
declares the Lord, "I will not be angry for ever.
13 Only acknowledge your guilt – you have rebelled
against the Lord your God, you have scattered your
favours to foreign gods under every spreading tree,
and have not obeyed me,"' declares the Lord.*

And then
Jeremiah 15:6
*6 You have rejected me,' declares the Lord. 'You
keep on backsliding. So I will reach out and destroy
you; I am tired of holding back.*

It is also valuable to note that even when God told
Israel to go to war against those who threatened to
annihilate them or overwhelm them or threaten
their faith, he set ethical limits unlike other warring
nations.

Deuteronomy 20
Going to War
*20 When you go to war against your enemies and
see horses and chariots and an army greater than
yours, do not be afraid of them, because the Lord*

your God, who brought you up out of Egypt, will be with you. ....5 The officers shall say to the army: "Has anyone built a new house and not yet begun to live in it? Let him go home, or he may die in battle and someone else may begin to live in it. 6 Has anyone planted a vineyard and not begun to enjoy it? Let him go home, or he may die in battle and someone else enjoy it. 7 Has anyone become pledged to a woman and not married her? Let him go home, or he may die in battle and someone else marry her." 8 Then the officers shall add, "Is anyone afraid or fainthearted? Let him go home so that his fellow soldiers will not become disheartened too............................

10 When you march up to attack a city, <u>make its people an offer of peace</u>. 11 If they accept and open their gates, all the people in it shall be subject to forced labour and shall work for you.

CONCLUSION: God created the world and then chose a particular nation to work through to ensure the world knew about him, his commandments, his nature and his plans for the Messiah.

Nothing would stop God from doing what he intended to do, not a people who went away from their faith, nor any enemies who would try to destroy that faith.

That God, as well as being a God of love is a God of Justice, who carries out his promises whatever the cost, can seem shocking.

However, considering the logic can it be a sound reason for saying he doesn't exist?

Chapter 12

Why does God allow suffering if he is a God of love?

This is a difficult and complex question and cannot be answered completely because we eventually arrive at the limit of what we can know.

It is also a subject which should not be discussed with anyone who is going through a time of suffering, perhaps bereavement or serious illness. At those times theological explanations are unhelpful, sympathy, compassion and words of comfort are what is required.

However when we are in a situation of being able to consider and discuss the issue of suffering objectively, theologians have, down the years, have helped us by providing some very helpful possible explanations.

Firstly suffering can be defined as: 'The state of undergoing pain, distress, or hardship'.

The Bible tells us that:

a) Suffering is caused by evil
b) Evil existed before the creation of the Earth
c) God did not want the knowledge of evil to enter the human condition, but mankind (Adam and Eve) allowed it in through disobeying God.

Why, we might ask would God allow mankind the choice. The answer is he wanted a relationship based upon love not compulsion. So he created humans with free will and reasoning powers so that they could choose him or reject him. True love cannot exist between two people if there is no freedom to choose.

Theologians have classified evil and resultant suffering into two forms:

Natural Evil and Moral Evil.

Natural evil, is the evil which causes suffering to humans but which is not due to the behaviour of other humans. This includes natural disasters like tsunamis, earthquakes, drought, and famine, and also disease.

Moral evil, is evil that is caused by human behaviour. Murder, rape, robbery, fraud, hatred, cheating, stealing. Jealousy, violence, racialism, apathy etc. When people, choose to act in defiance of God's laws, the result is moral evil.

Looking at the definition of suffering again: 'The state of undergoing pain, distress, or hardship', a perusal of government and charity statistics shows that suffering due to human behaviour massively outweighs suffering due to natural disasters and serious illness. That means that when we ask; why does God allow suffering? The biggest part of the answer is because he allows each of us to choose how we behave, and if we behaved as he wanted suffering would be massively reduced.

Theological explanations

There are a huge number of books and studies on this subject but most of them trace their basic principles back to one of two theologians.

Augustine: (354- 430 AD)

The theologian St. Augustine suggested that all suffering is due to the Fall of Humanity after the disobedience in the Garden of Eden. He proposed that, humankind is responsible for evil by being led astray by Satan. This absolves God, of creating evil.

Irenaeus (130-202 AD) proposed that the existence of evil actually serves a purpose. For example it could be used by God to mentor and discipline Christians to becoming good people.

Leibneitz the famous mathematician (1676-1714) suggested that God had chosen the best possible design for the world out of an infinite number of possibilities. The argument being that if God is all powerful, all knowing, and all loving, then the creation we have is the best one for us, even if that includes the mystery of suffering.

The arguments of Irenaeus and Leibnitz may sound challenging but some phenomenon can sometimes suggest suffering has a purpose.

For example:
When God's commandments are broken there are usually some negative consequences and that can cause us to consider a change of behaviour or attitude.

Suffering pain can often be an early warning that something is beginning and we need to seek medical advice. Responding to this pain warning can save our life.

The parent who deeply loves a child will subject them to suffering through discipline in order to stop them developing bad characteristics, like telling lies for example.

Humans 'kill' (cause suffering) plants and animals in order to eat.

It is also interesting to note that many Christian virtues can only be practised if someone is suffering and has needs, for example; care, compassion, sympathy, empathy, charity, forgiveness, patience. etc.

Chapter 13

Why would a loving God make rules about sex and sexuality?

It is clear from the bible that gender and sexual relationships were a fundamental building block of God's plan of creation.

Whether you believe the creation story literally or not, it begins, in the book of Genesis with God having created man, and then immediately saying 'it is not good for him to be alone' in other words the man needed company. So God created woman, he did so in such a biological way, that not only could they express their love for each other through the joy of sex, this act itself would be the means of procreation.

Before long we find that in the book of Leviticus forms of sexual relationships other than that described above were occurring, and God issued decrees condemning them. That is the sexual acts not the people engaged in them.

These condemned acts include adultery, rape, incest and some forms of same sex sexual acts, which have been translated as meaning homosexuality. The word homosexual did not appear in Bible translations until 1946, the original King James Version using the phrase 'Thou shalt not lie with mankind, as with womankind'. Some scholars argue that these and other Old Testament references to homosexuality are made in the context condemning sex acts used as part of idol worship involving male prostitutes, and do not refer to loving relationships between consenting adults.

Other Bible scholars challenge this view by pointing to other bible verses such as those in the New Testament. (Romans, Corinthians and Timothy.) Which they argue clearly describe same sex sexual relations as sinful or not in accordance with God's order of creation. Some quote the following verses as evidence, that Jesus' held this view.

Matthew 19:4-6

4 "Haven't you read," he replied, "that at the beginning the Creator 'made them male and female,' 5 and said, 'For this reason a man will leave his father and mother and be united to his wife, and the two will become one flesh'? 6 So they

are no longer two, but one flesh. Therefore what God has joined together, let no one separate."

In summary it is clear that the Old Testament laws consider same sex sexual acts as forbidden in the context of rape, promiscuity and ritualistic idol worship, but some scholars argue this does not relate to loving relationships between two consenting people. Others argue that God's created order, and word, assumes that sexual acts should only occur between a man and a woman who are married.

Sexual sin in context
The word sin literally means to 'miss the target' and could be used to describe the action of an archer whose arrow failed to hit the bull's eye of a target. In human terms it means failing to live and act as God wants us to. The problem is that everyone sins, as the Bible says
Romans 3:23
23 for all have sinned and fall short of the glory of God, 24and all are justified freely by his grace through the redemption that came by Christ Jesus.

The good news is that we can receive forgiveness through the grace of God (More about this in a later chapter).

CS Lewis a famous scholar and Christian author puts sexual sin in context, in his book 'Mere Christianity' as follows:
 "The Great Sin" from "Mere Christianity" by C.S. Lewis
"I now come to that part of Christian morals where they differ most sharply from all other morals. There is one vice of which no man in the world is free; which everyone in the world loathes when he sees it in someone else' and of which hardly any people, except Christians, ever imagine that they are guilty themselves. I have heard people admit that they are bad tempered, or that they cannot keep their heads about girls or drink, or even that they are cowards. I do not think I have ever heard anyone who was not a Christian accuse himself of this vice. And at the same time I have very seldom met anyone, who was not a Christian, who showed the slightest mercy to it in others. There is no fault which makes a man more unpopular, and no fault

which we are more unconscious of in ourselves.
And the more we have it ourselves, the more we
dislike it in others.
The vice I am talking of is Pride or Self-Conceit: and
the virtue opposite to it, in Christian morals, is
called Humility. You may remember, when I was
talking about sexual morality, I warned you that
the centre of Christian morals did not lie there.
Well, now, we have come to the centre……………"

John 3:16
16 For God so loved the world that he gave his one
and only Son, that whoever believes in him shall
not perish but have eternal life.

I have had the privilege of having some gay people
attend my course discussion groups.
We concluded that once they had found faith, it
was for them to begin a relationship with God to
enjoy his grace, and listen to his voice.
And to develop a deeper relationship with God:
and this was the path they chose.

Chapter 14

Who was Jesus and what evidence is there, that he existed?

Jesus Outside the bible

'Jesus Christ is the only proof of the living God. We only know God through Jesus Christ'.

- Blaise Pascal French mathematician and Philosopher.

'There was no such person in the history of the world as Jesus Christ. There was no historical, living, breathing, sentient human being by that name. Ever. The Bible is a fictional, non-historical narrative'.

- Jon Murray, President American Atheists

The Facts

More information has survived about Jesus Christ than most other ancient figures. Yet few historical persons have ever had their existence so questioned and researched.

One result of all that research is that information about Jesus Christ, from sources other than the Bible, is readily accessible to anyone interested.

Unfortunately, this information for some reason is not well publicised or known about. This is perhaps because almost any material with significant reference to Jesus Christ may be classified as religious or even proselytising and therefore does not appear in educational books, or institutional documents. However the evidence for the life of Jesus Christ in secular historical records and books is very substantial.

Testimonies from hostile sources.

Hostile sources are considered to be those historians, politicians and writers, who were definitely not followers of Jesus; i.e., people who clearly were not out to promote favourable belief in him.

The fact that hostile sources describe the activities and influence of Jesus, as well as other New Testament characters and events, is evidence for both the existence of Christ and the accuracy of the Bible record.

It follows that although these 'hostile' writers wrote what they witnessed, this does not mean they were believers, and therefore their accounts of the life and works of Jesus are not always positive.

The Sources

JOSEPHUS

Josephus was a Jewish historian who was born around AD 38. He was initially a commander of part of the Jewish forces fighting against the army of Rome. In 67 CE being surrounded by Roman forces he surrendered and was absorbed into the Roman establishment. Later when Vespasian became emperor, Josephus was appointed as his court historian. In AD 93, Josephus wrote a historical account of the Jews entitled 'Antiquities of the Jews'. In his account several passages confirm events described in the Bible and the life of Jesus and John the Baptist, as follows:

a) *'But to some of the Jews the destruction of Herod's army seemed to be divine vengeance, and certainly a just vengeance, for his treatment of John, surnamed the Baptist. For Herod had put him to death, though he was a good man and had exhorted the Jews to lead righteous lives, to practice justice towards their fellows and piety towards God, and so doing to join in baptism.'*

b) *...convened the judges of the Sanhedrin and brought before them a man named James, the brother of Jesus who was called the Christ, and certain others. He accused them of having transgressed the law and delivered them up to be stoned.*

c) At this time there was a wise man who was called Jesus. And his conduct was good, and [he] was known to be virtuous. And many people from among the Jews and the other nations became his disciples. Pilate condemned him to be crucified and to die. And those who had become his disciples did not abandon his discipleship. They reported that he had appeared to them three days after his crucifixion and that he was alive;

Pliny the Younger (AD 61-113)

Pliny was the Roman governor of Bithynia. He was also a lawyer, author, and magistrate .He wrote hundreds of letters to officials and politicians, many of which have survived. One example is a letter he wrote to the Roman Emperor Trajan around AD112. This letter speaks about the followers of Jesus whom Pliny was obliged by law to hunt down and execute them. He writes as follows:

In the meantime, the method I have observed towards those who have been denounced to me as

Christians is this: I interrogated them whether they were in fact Christians; if they confessed it, I repeated the question twice, adding the threat of capital punishment; if they still persevered, I ordered them to be executed.

They affirmed, however, that the whole of their guilt, or their error, was that they were in the habit of meeting on a certain fixed day before it was light, when they sang in alternate verses a hymn to Christ, as to a god, and bound themselves by a solemn oath, not to perform any wicked deed, never to commit any fraud, theft or adultery, never to falsify their word, nor deny a trust when they should be called upon to make it good; after which it was their custom to separate, and then reassemble to partake of food - but food of an ordinary and innocent kind.

TACITUS (AD 56- 120)

Tacitus was a Roman historian and politician. He is considered to be one of the greatest Roman historians. Tacitus was a senator in Rome and later a governor of Asia. Around AD 116 he wrote an account of a fire which swept Rome at the time of the Emperor Nero in Ad 64, as follows:

Consequently, to get rid of the report, Nero fastened the guilt and inflicted the most exquisite tortures on a class hated for their abominations, called Christians by the populace. Christus (Jesus), from whom the name had its origin, suffered the extreme penalty during the reign of Tiberius at the hands of one of our procurators, Pontius Pilate, and a most mischievous superstition thus checked for the moment, again broke out not only in Judea, the first source of the evil, but even in Rome...

SUETONIUS (69-122AD)

Suetonius was a Roman historian, and secretary to Emperor Hadrian. Around AD129 he wrote an account of the life of Claudius in which he stated

Because the Jews at Rome caused continuous disturbances at the instigation of Chrestus (Jesus), he expelled them from the city.

LUCIAN (c. 125 – 180)

Lucian was a writer and satirist who was well known for ridiculing religions. In AD170 he wrote the following in his work 'The Death of Peregrine'.

The Christians, you know, worship a man to this day - the distinguished personage who introduced their novel rites, and was crucified on that account... You see, these misguided creatures start with the general conviction that they are immortal for all time, which explains the contempt of death and voluntary self-devotion which are so common among them; and then it was impressed upon them by their original lawgiver that they are all brothers, from the moment that they are converted, and deny the gods of Greece, and worship the crucified sage, and live after his laws.

THE TALMUD

The Talmud is a collection of Jewish history passed down orally and was put into writing around AD70. One section includes the following:

On the eve of Passover they hanged Yeshu (Jesus). And an announcer went out, in front of him, for forty days (saying): 'He is going to be stoned because he practiced sorcery and enticed and led Israel astray. Anyone who knows anything in his favour, let him come and plead in his behalf.' But, not having found anything in his favour, they hanged him on the eve of the Passover.

This description of be led by an announcer seeking witnesses for defence is in keeping with Jewish legal process of the time

SUMMARY

The testimonies of martyrs

Jesus' disciples and members of the early church were persecuted and many executed.

In the Roman Empire all an individual had to do to escape death was to renounce belief in Jesus, as described here by Pliny the Roman Governor in a letter to his superior.

Those who denied they were, or had ever been, Christians, and who repeated after me an invocation to the gods,... and who finally cursed Christ - none of which acts, it is said, those who are really Christians can be forced into performing - these I thought it proper to discharge.

Tacitus the historian also records, at the time of Emperor Nero, the fate of Christians who refused to deny Jesus:

Mockery of every sort was added to their deaths. Covered with the skins of beasts, they were torn by dogs and perished, or were nailed to crosses, or were doomed to the flames and burnt, to serve as a nightly illumination, when daylight had expired.

Historians believe that about 3500 Christians were put to death in this way. Considering all they had to do to save themselves was to renounce Jesus, this is surely a powerful piece of evidence that Jesus lived, was considered divine, and his followers, many of whom were eye witnesses would rather die than see faith in him lost or destroyed.

Chapter 15

Accepting the evidence that Jesus did exists how can we know he was who he claimed to be?

"Mad, Bad, or God"

How can we know if Jesus was who he claimed to be, namely the son of God, or God incarnate. CS Lewis the Oxford professor and writer suggested that once you examine the evidence in the Bible you are left with only three possibilities. These are that Jesus was either mad, bad or God.

'Then comes the real shock. Among these Jews there suddenly turns up a man who goes about talking as if he was God. He claims to forgive sins. He says He has always existed. He says He is coming to judge the world at the end of time....I am trying here to prevent anyone saying the really foolish thing that people often say about Him: 'I'm ready to accept Jesus as a great moral teacher, but I don't accept his claim to be God.' That is the one thing we must not say. A man who was merely a man and said the sort of things Jesus said would not be a great moral teacher. He would be either a lunatic—on a level with the man who says he is a poached egg—or else he would be the Devil in Hell. You must make your choice. Either this man was, and is, the Son of God: or else a madman or something worse.' CS Lewis, Mere Christianity

Was Jesus Mad?

Several famous psychiatrists have tried to carry out a retrospective analysis of Jesus through his sayings and actions. The outcomes of these vary from favourable to unfavourable, and possibly reflect the original beliefs of the individual.

On one level if you do not believe in God at all, and you have a friend who does, and prays out loud to God, and believes he receives answers, you may consider him or her 'a bit odd', even deranged. On the other hand would you not look for other evidence in this persons' behaviour and life to make a judgement on if they were sane or not.

It is interesting to note that Jesus's family did exactly that. Jesus had four brothers and two sisters. In his early ministry when reports came back to them that Jesus behaving strangely and challenging religious leaders, they became concerned.

Mark 3:21
Then Jesus entered a house, and again a crowd gathered, so that he and his disciples were not even able to eat. 21 When his family heard about this, they went to take charge of him, for they said, 'He is out of his mind.'...........

We are not told what happened next, but if you were told your brother was acting strangely and you went to listen to him, your following actions would surely show what conclusion you had come to. Well in the case of Jesus' brothers they showed they believed he was who he said he was.
His brother James became the leader of the church in Jerusalem and wrote the book of James in the New Testament. His brother Jude, also became a

believer and authored the New Testament book that bears his name. Bear in mind also that they were eye witnesses to the life and death of Jesus. After the ressurection of Jesus the Bible tells us that Mary the mother of Jesus and his brothers were part of the disciples group.

Acts 1:*14 They all joined together constantly in prayer, along with the women and Mary the mother of Jesus, and with his brothers.*

Would Jesus' mother and brothers join in prayers to him if they did not believe he was the son of God? It is implausible that they would pray to him if they thought he was just mad. They also of course had witnessed his ressurection.

Was Jesus Bad?

In the same biblical account that we read above when Jesus' family came to find him, we are told that local religious leaders in his audience were angry with him.

They said that the miracles he had performed were of 'witchcraft' of 'evil spirits' and accused him of being under the Devil's influence.

This clearly indicates they had seen something miraculous they could not explain.

With regard as to whether Jesus was evil or not needs little investigation. His life and works were all of sacrificial goodness, and he spoke against the works of the Devil and personally resisted him.

Was Jesus who he said he was?

Putting aside the evidence of personal faith that millions down the centuries have experienced, there is also much in the Bible to confirm that Jesus was the promised Messiah and son of God.

One of the most powerful pieces of evidence is the hundreds of prophecies made about the coming of the Messiah which were fullfilled by Jesus.

Prophecies fulfilled by Jesus

Book of Daniel

There are over 350 prophecies in the Bible written hundreds of years before that were fulfilled by Jesus.

The prophecy in the book of Daniel is often quoted as an example because it is impressive in that it prophecies dates so accurately. It is not detailed here as it does require a reasonable amount of Biblical knowledge to understand it but there are many books which explain it in detail

He will be born of a virgin   Isaiah 7:

Fulfilment:
Matthew 1:20-23
20 But after he had considered this, an angel of the Lord appeared to him in a dream and said, 'Joseph son of David, do not be afraid to take Mary home as your wife, because what is conceived in her is

from the Holy Spirit. 21 She will give birth to a son, and you are to give him the name Jesus, because he will save his people from their sins.'

22 All this took place to fulfil what the Lord had said through the prophet: 23 'The virgin will conceive and give birth to a son, and they will call him Immanuel' (which means 'God with us').

He will be born in Bethlehem   Micah 5:2

Fulfilment:
Matthew 2: 1-6
After Jesus was born in Bethlehem in Judea, during the time of King Herod, Magi from the east came to Jerusalem ² and asked, 'Where is the one who has been born king of the Jews? We saw his star when it rose and have come to worship him.'³ When King Herod heard this he was disturbed, and all Jerusalem with him. ⁴ When he had called together all the people's chief priests and teachers of the law, he asked them where the Messiah was to be born. ⁵ 'In Bethlehem in Judea,' they replied, 'for this is what the prophet has written: "But you, Bethlehem, in the land of Judah, are by no means

*least among the rulers of Judah; for out of you will
come a ruler who will shepherd my people Israel."*

**He will be a Prophet, King and priest
Deuteronomy 18:15**

Fulfilment:
*John 7:40-42
40 On hearing his words, some of the people said,
'Surely this man is the Prophet.'
41 Others said, 'He is the Messiah.'
Still others asked, 'How can the Messiah come from
Galilee? 42 Does not Scripture say that the Messiah
will come from David's descendants and from
Bethlehem, the town where David lived?*

*Matthew 21:8-11
8 A very large crowd spread their cloaks on the
road, while others cut branches from the trees and
spread them on the road. 9 The crowds that went
ahead of him and those that followed shouted,
'Hosanna to the Son of David!'
'Blessed is he who comes in the name of the Lord!
'Hosanna in the highest heaven!'*

123

10 When Jesus entered Jerusalem, the whole city was stirred and asked, 'Who is this?'
11 The crowds answered, 'This is Jesus, the prophet from Nazareth in Galilee.'

He will be tempted by Satan   Psalm 91:10-12

Fulfilment:
Matthew 4:1-11
1Then Jesus was led by the Spirit into the wilderness to be tempted by the devil. 2 After fasting for forty days and forty nights, he was hungry. 3 The tempter came to him and said, 'If you are the Son of God, tell these stones to become bread.'4 Jesus answered, 'It is written: "Man shall not live on bread alone, but on every word that comes from the mouth of God."

He will enter Jerusalem Triumphantly   Zechariah 9:9
Fulfilment:
Luke 19:35-37. 35 They brought it to Jesus, threw their cloaks on the colt and put Jesus on it. 36 As he went along, people spread their cloaks on the road.

37 When he came near the place where the road goes down the Mount of Olives, the whole crowd of disciples began joyfully to praise God in loud voices for all the miracles they had seen:

He will be rejected by his own people   Isaiah 53:1

Fulfilment:
John 1:10-11
10 He was in the world, and though the world was made through him, the world did not recognise him. 11 He came to that which was his own, but his own did not receive him.

John 12:37-38
37 Even after Jesus had performed so many signs in their presence, they still would not believe in him. 38 This was to fulfil the word of Isaiah the prophet: 'Lord, who has believed our message and to whom has the arm of the Lord been revealed?'

He will be betrayed by one of his followers
Psalm 41:

**He will be betrayed for thirty pieces of silver
Zechariah 11:12-13**

Fulfilment:
Matthew 26:14-28
*14 Then one of the Twelve – the one called Judas
Iscariot – went to the chief priests 15 and asked,
'What are you willing to give me if I deliver him
over to you?' So they counted out for him thirty
pieces of silver. 16 From then on Judas watched for
an opportunity to hand him over.*

He will be tried and condemned   Isaiah 53:8

Fulfilment:
Matthew 27:1-2
*Early in the morning, all the chief priests and the
elders of the people made their plans how to have
Jesus executed. 2 So they bound him, led him away
and handed him over to Pilate the governor.*

**He will be silent before his accusers   Psalm 35:11:
Fulfilment:**
Matthew 27:12-14

12 When he was accused by the chief priests and the elders, he gave no answer. 13 Then Pilate asked him, 'Don't you hear the testimony they are bringing against you?' 14 But Jesus made no reply, not even to a single charge – to the great amazement of the governor.

He will be crucified   Psalm 22:14
Fulfilment:
   John 19:4-6
4 Once more Pilate came out and said to the Jews gathered there, 'Look, I am bringing him out to you to let you know that I find no basis for a charge against him.' 5 When Jesus came out wearing the crown of thorns and the purple robe, Pilate said to them, 'Here is the man!'
6 As soon as the chief priests and their officials saw him, they shouted, 'Crucify! Crucify!'
These are but a few of the hundreds of prophesies that Jesus fullfilled. It has been estimated by mathematicians that the probability that Jesus could have fulfilled even just eight of the 350 he fullfilled would be
1 in 100, 000, 000, 000, 000, 000.

Chapter 16

Assuming Jesus does exists what is his relevance to me today?

In order to understand the life claims and significance of Jesus you have to read the Bible's account of his life. A good place to start is Mark's gospel which is the shortest gospel, and gives an overview.
Matthew and Lukes Gospel provide a longer and more detailed read

The following summaries may give some helpful background before reading the Gospel of Mark

Summary of the Old Testament
In the beginning God created the earth and everything in it, and he was pleased with the creation and called it good.
In the sequence of creation God last of all created man (Adam and Eve).
Because he loved them so much he gave them complete free will to choose how they wanted to

live. Unfortunately they chose to listen to the voice
of evil (represented by the serpent in the Bible),
and in doing so allowed sin to enter into the world.
God was upset at this, and told them that as he
was a Holy God, he could not have a relationship
with them which included sinful behaviour as it
would end in disaster, and not the perfect creation
he intended.

God did not however destroy Adam and Eve and
start again but spoke of a plan to draw them back
to himself.
Some of the descendants of Adam and Eve were
what we know as the people of Israel the Jewish
race.

He told them through their leaders such as
Abraham and Moses, that he had chosen them to
be his people on earth, and he would use them to
spread knowledge of himself throughout the world.
That they may be worthy of such a role God made
a contract (covenant) with them.
This contract said that if the people of Israel
obeyed God's commandments and continued in

faith and the spreading of faith, he would bless them in many, many ways. The people of Israel agreed to this contract and swore their allegiance and obedience to God.

God reminded them however that he could not tolerate sin, and in fact such sinfulness deserved a death penalty. However in his mercy he told them that if they regularly confessed their sin and offered sacrifices he would not punish them.

The people of Israel populated the known world and took their faith with them as God had commanded.
However there were periods of great sinfulness and unbelief.

So God sent Prophets to warn the people of Israel about the consequences of breaking their contract.

He also used these prophets to tell them that he would as promised, bring forth a messiah through them, who would remove the burden of sin, and the need for punishment for sin for everyone for evermore. Jesus was that Messiah and His story is told in the New Testament.

Summary of the New Testament

The New Testament tells of the birth, life, teachings, death and ressurection of Jesus, and the history and teachings of the early churches.

Jesus' birth was miraculous, he came not only to teach, but also to live a life completely without sin. It was this perfection that made him the only person who could die and pay the price of sins for everyone.
 He was perfect yet was punished and sacrificed so that none of us needs to be punished for our sins.

The essence of the Bible is that it is sin that has corrupted the world and caused sadness, anxiety, unhappiness, and suffering for everyone.
Also personal unforgiven sin causes those same things in each individual.
Yes we can distract ourselves by hobbies, going out or whatever, but the only way to find true peace

and purpose is by accepting what Jesus Christ is offering.

Obviously in trying to sum up the Bible so briefly much is lost so joining a church discussion group such as the 'Alpha Courses' or similar is a great way learn more.

The teaching and invitations of Jesus

Reading a gospel as suggested will give you a full account of the teachings of Jesus. Here are some key passages which give a summary.

Who Jesus is
'But what about you?' he asked. 'Who do you say I am?'
16 Simon Peter answered, 'You are the Messiah, the Son of the living God.'
17 Jesus replied, 'Blessed are you, Simon son of Jonah, for this was not revealed to you by flesh and blood, but by my Father in heaven. Matthew 16:15-17

For God so loved the world that he gave his one and only Son, that whoever believes in him shall not perish but have eternal life. John 3:16

His invitations to us

'Come to me, all you who are weary and burdened, and I will give you rest. 29 Take my yoke upon you and learn from me, for I am gentle and humble in heart, and you will find rest for your souls. 30 For my yoke is easy and my burden is light.' Matthew 11:28-30

Jesus answered, 'I am the way and the truth and the life. No one comes to the Father except through me. John 14:6

Whoever believes and is baptized will be saved, but whoever does not believe will be condemned. Mark 16:16

25 Jesus said to her, "I am the resurrection and the life. The one who believes in me will live, even though they die; 26 and whoever lives by believing in me will never die. Do you believe this?" John 11:25-26

The Blessings that follow

'I have told you these things, so that in me you may have peace. In this world you will have trouble. But take heart! I have overcome the world.' John 16:33

5 'I am the vine; you are the branches. If you remain in me and I in you, you will bear much fruit; apart from me you can do nothing.................9 'As the Father has loved me, so have I loved you. Now remain in my love. 10 If you keep my commands, you will remain in my love, just as I have kept my Father's commands and remain in his love. 11 I have told you this so that my joy may be in you and that your joy may be complete.
Matthew 15:5-11
Therefore, if anyone is in Christ, the new creation has come: the old has gone, the new is here!
2 Corinthians 5:17

I told you that you would die in your sins; if you do not believe that I am he, you will indeed die in your sins.'
John 8:24

Matthew 5 (The Message Bible)
When Jesus saw his ministry drawing huge crowds, he climbed a hillside. Those who were apprenticed to him, the committed, climbed with him. Arriving at a quiet place, he sat down and taught his climbing companions.

This is what he said:
3 "You're blessed when you're at the end of your rope. With less of you there is more of God and his rule.
4 "You're blessed when you feel you've lost what is most dear to you. Only then can you be embraced by the One most dear to you.
5 "You're blessed when you're content with just who you are—no more, no less. That's the moment you find yourselves proud owners of everything that can't be bought.

6 "You're blessed when you've worked up a good appetite for God. He's food and drink in the best meal you'll ever eat.
7 "You're blessed when you care. At the moment of being 'care-full,' you find yourselves cared for.

8 "You're blessed when you get your inside world—your mind and heart—put right. Then you can see God in the outside world.

9 "You're blessed when you can show people how to cooperate instead of compete or fight. That's when you discover who you really are, and your place in God's family.

10 "You're blessed when your commitment to God provokes persecution. The persecution drives you even deeper into God's kingdom.

11-12 "Not only that—count yourselves blessed every time people put you down or throw you out or speak lies about you to discredit me. What it means is that the truth is too close for comfort and they are uncomfortable. You can be glad when that happens— give a cheer, even!—for though they don't like it, I do! And all heaven applauds. And know that you are in good company. My prophets and witnesses have always gotten into this kind of trouble.

13 "Let me tell you why you are here. You're here to be salt-seasoning that brings out the God-flavours of this earth. If you lose your saltiness, how will people taste godliness? You've lost your usefulness and will end up in the garbage.

14-16 "Here's another way to put it: You're here to be light, bringing out the God-colours in the world. God is not a secret to be kept. We're going public with this, as public as a city on a hill. If I make you light-bearers, you don't think I'm going to hide you under a bucket, do you? I'm putting you on a light stand. Now that I've put you there on a hilltop, on a light stand—shine! Keep open house; be generous with your lives. By opening up to others, you'll prompt people to open up with God, this generous Father in heaven. Matthew 5 (The Message)

Chapter 17

How do you become a Christian?

To repeat an illustration used earlier.
Suppose you come home early one day and you are not sure if any of the family is at home.
As you enter the front door you call out 'Is anyone at home?
You may or may not get an answer, however you thought it was enough of a possibility to ask the question.
In the same way if you want to know if God exists, the simplest way to find out is to make your own enquiry. It simply requires enough belief in the possibility as it did in the illustration above.
Jesus said, that if you have faith which is only the size of a mustard seed you can move mountains.

Many atheists seem to fail to understand this point at all. They assume that those who believe in God do so through intellectual assent alone.

They argue that believers have 'misunderstood' the evidence and have therefore drawn false conclusions.

Arguments rage about evolution, creation etc. yet this completely fails to understand the basis of faith experienced by millions of people.

Belief may well begin to be stirred by the evidence around us, or some experience of some kind. Such observation and the reasoning from it, is for many people is a basis of their agnosticism.

However no rational person makes a life changing commitment to believe in God simply by what they observe in nature or physics.
Believers have far more concrete evidence than that, they believe they have enquired if God is there, and are convinced they have received an answer.

For believers this experience is not an isolated one, but one that is repeated over and over again. It is this repeated experience that convinces the believer of God's existence and not the analysis of competing theories of creation and evolution etc.

In fact most believers would describe their experiences as having a relationship with God.

Logical Proof through a relationship with God

So going back to where we started that our journey begins with the hypothesis that God may exist
A hypothesis being 'a theory needing investigation: a tentative explanation for a phenomenon, used as a basis for further investigation'

Well a hypothesis is usually written in two parts, a statement with an explanation following it. In the form of saying If X is true then, then Y will result.

So here are a string of hypotheses that can be considered sequentially.

1) If the bible's claims are true, God exists

2) If the bible's claims are true, I can only receive proof through faith

3) If the bible's claims are true, accepting the possibility of God is enough faith to begin

4) If the bible's claims are true, making a prayer admitting faith will cause God to respond

5) If the bible's claims are true Jesus is the son of God

6) If the claims of Jesus are true, becoming a Christian will transform my life and demonstrate the reality of God to me

7) If the bible's claims are true, on becoming a Christian I will have an inner peace and joy that I have never previously experienced

8) If the bible's claims are true becoming a Christian I will have an understanding of the world and its future which is rational and full of hope

9) If the bible's claims are true becoming a Christian, I will have a sense of purpose,

and understand the point of my
existence
10) If the bible's claims are true becoming a
Christian I will have a sense of
forgiveness and freedom from guilt and
the promise of eternal life

**So what does the Bible ask us to do in order to receive
a blessed life here on earth and an eternal life?**

Romans 10:9... if you declare with your mouth,
'Jesus is Lord,' and believe in your heart that God
raised him from the dead, you will be saved.

So to believe and then confess you belief is done by
making a prayer to God, in your own words.

To many people joining a discussion group such as
Alpha or a church discussion group is a massive
help in answering questions and finding out how to
pray.

Chapter 18

Your decision your future; what to do next

Finding a Church

It can be a bit confusing when you consider joining a church or discussion group. There are many different churches or denominations but in the main they believe and teach the same things. The differences are mainly to do with the style of worship (modern or traditional for example) and the way they are organised. Some denominations have plural leadership, others a single minister, some involve all members who vote on major decision.

Trying a course like Alpha or similar

All welcoming churches will have a discussion group such as Alpha, Emmaus, Christianity Explored, or similar.

These groups are open to believers and non- believers alike and simply provide an opportunity to investigate the Christian faith. There is absolutely no obligation with these 'courses' and you come and go as you please.

So in conclusion:

Does God exist?

Is the Bible truly the word of God?

Is Jesus who he claims to be?

Why not enquire?

Printed in Great Britain
by Amazon